DINOSAUR coloring book for kids Dinosaur Coloring Book for Boys, Girls, Toddlers, Preschoolers, Kids 3-8, 6-8

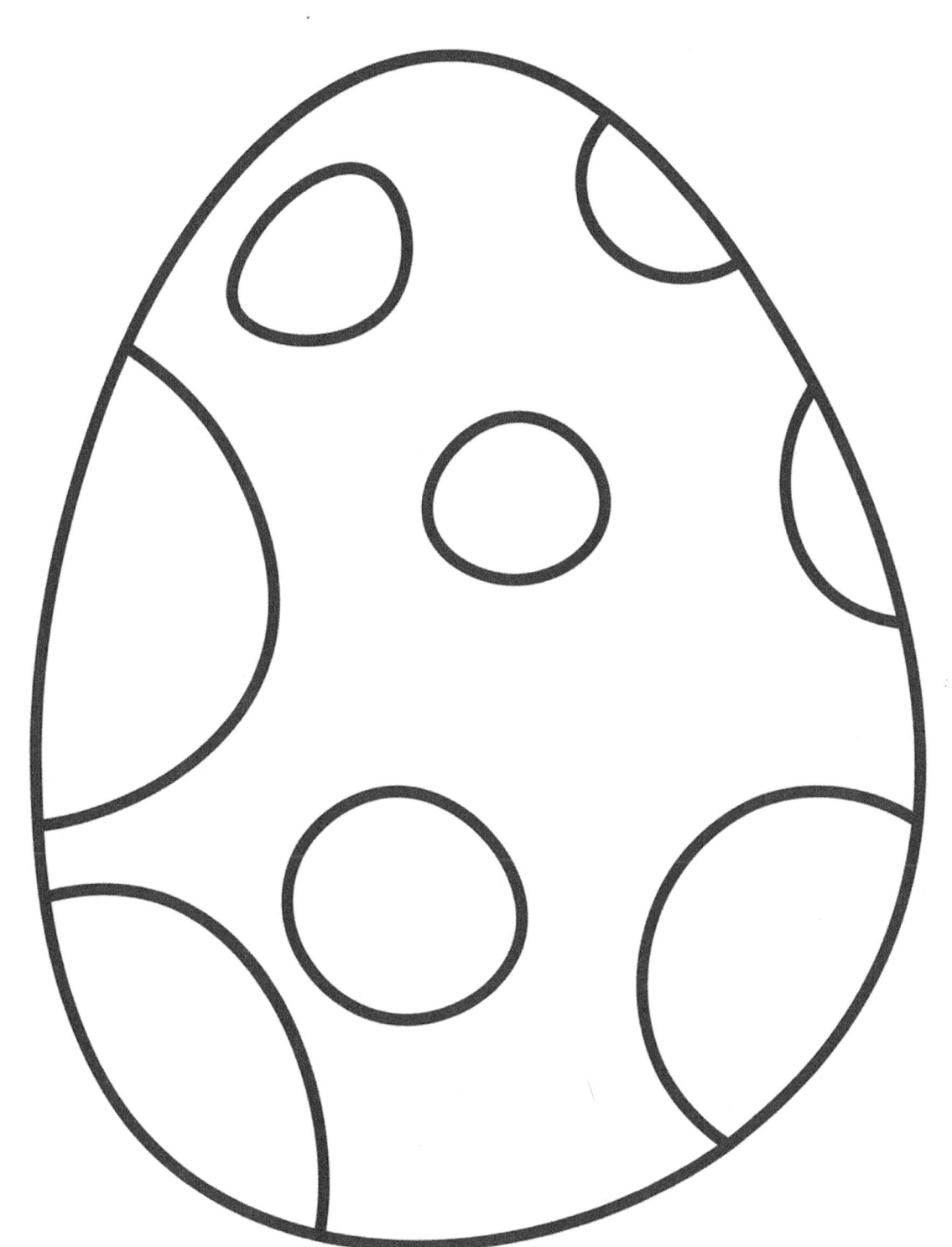

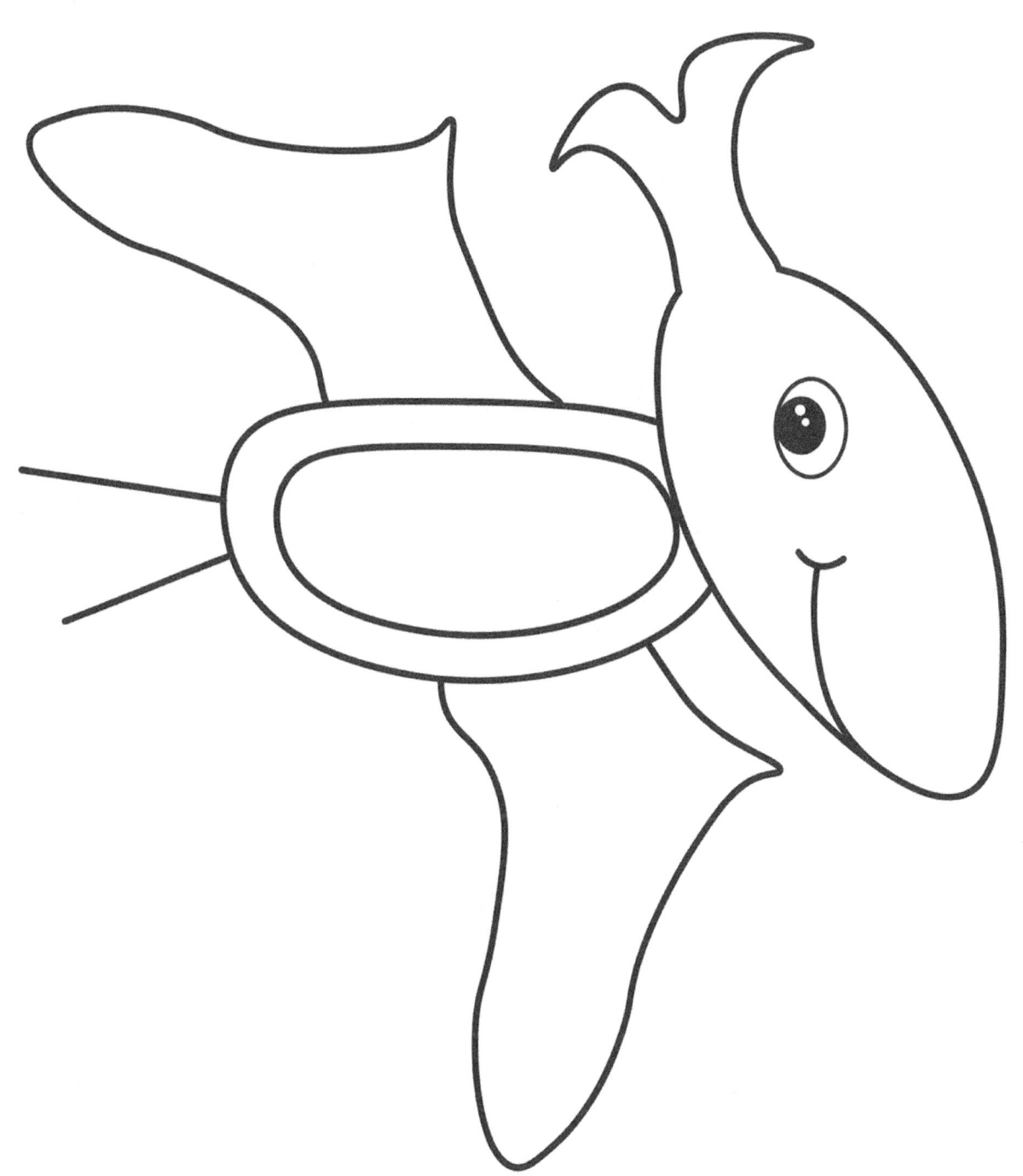

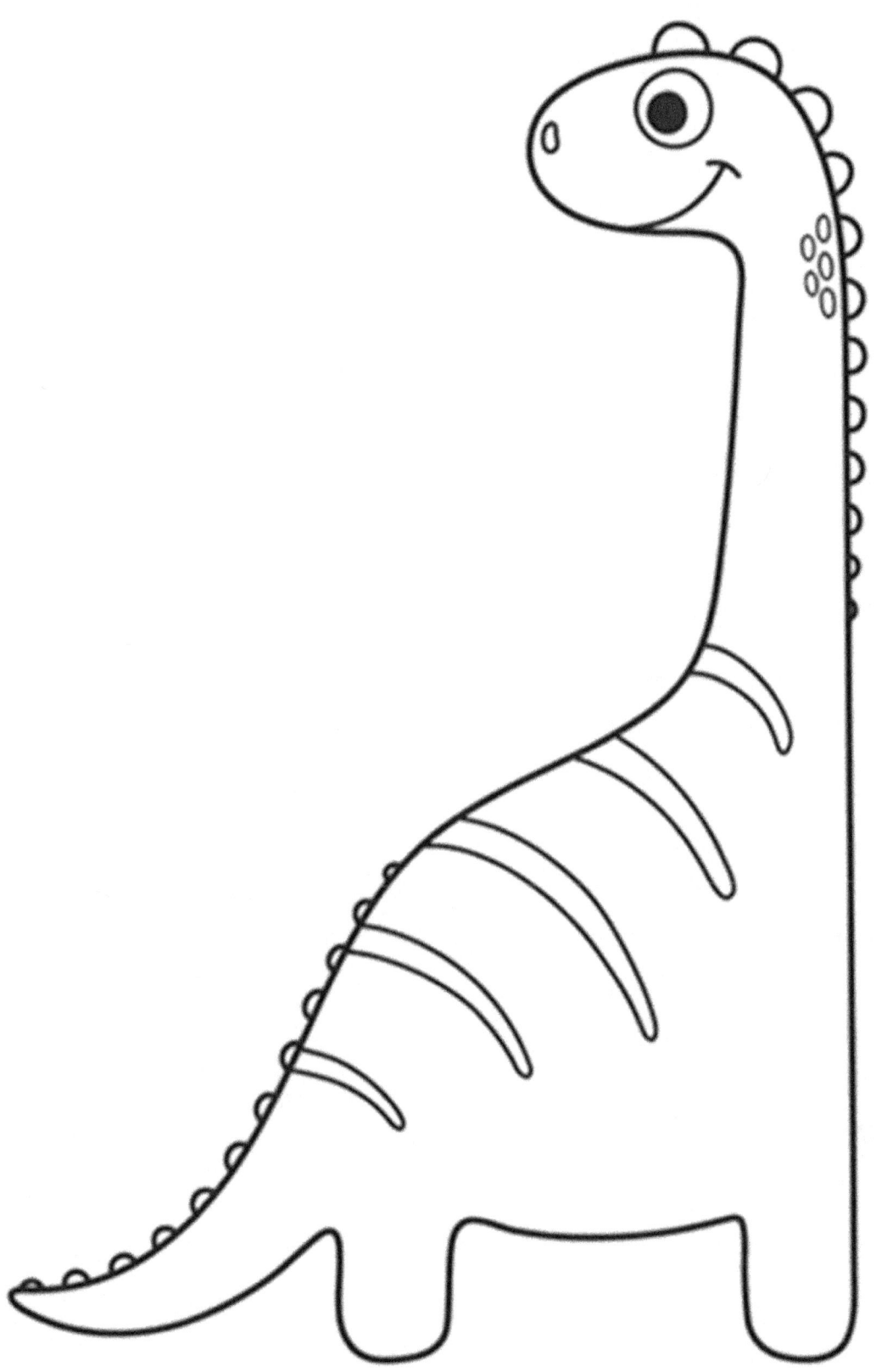

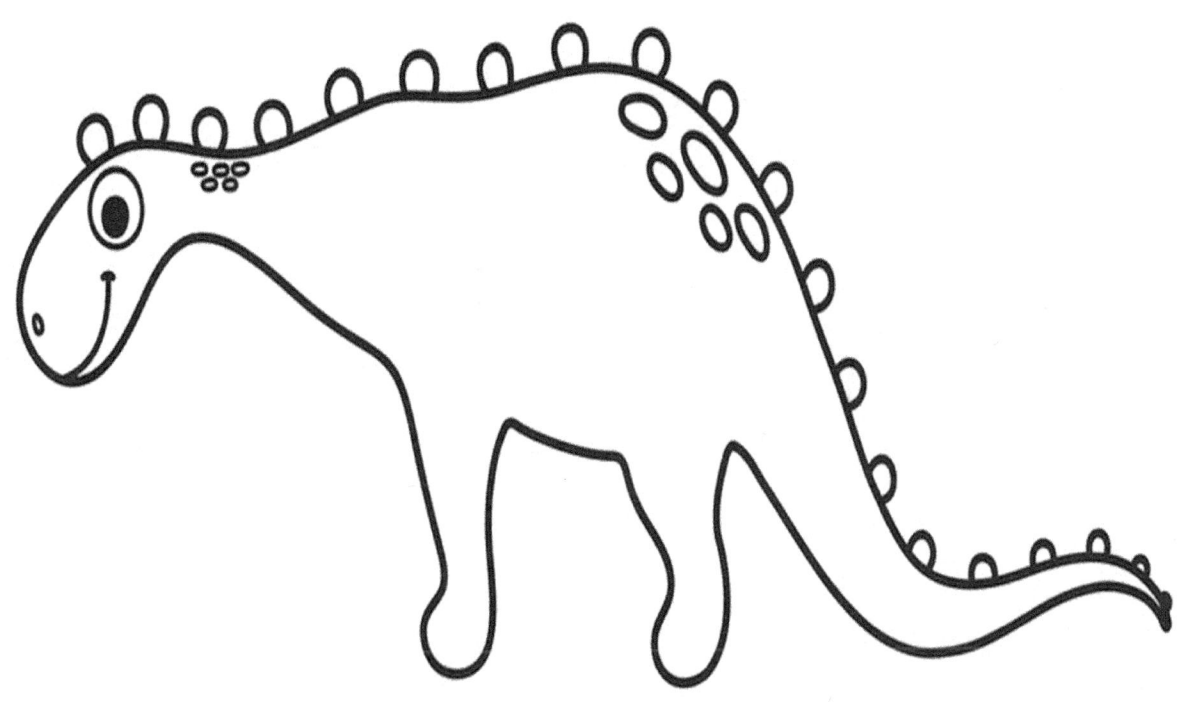

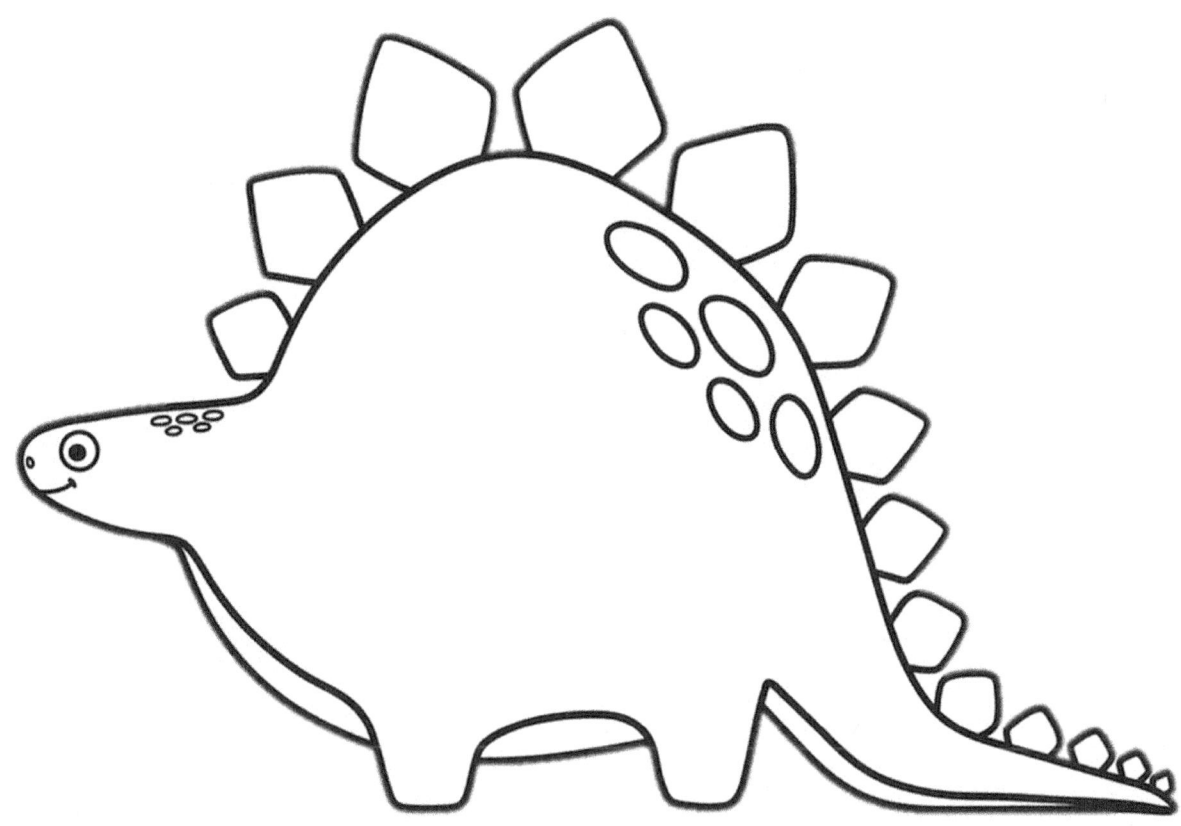

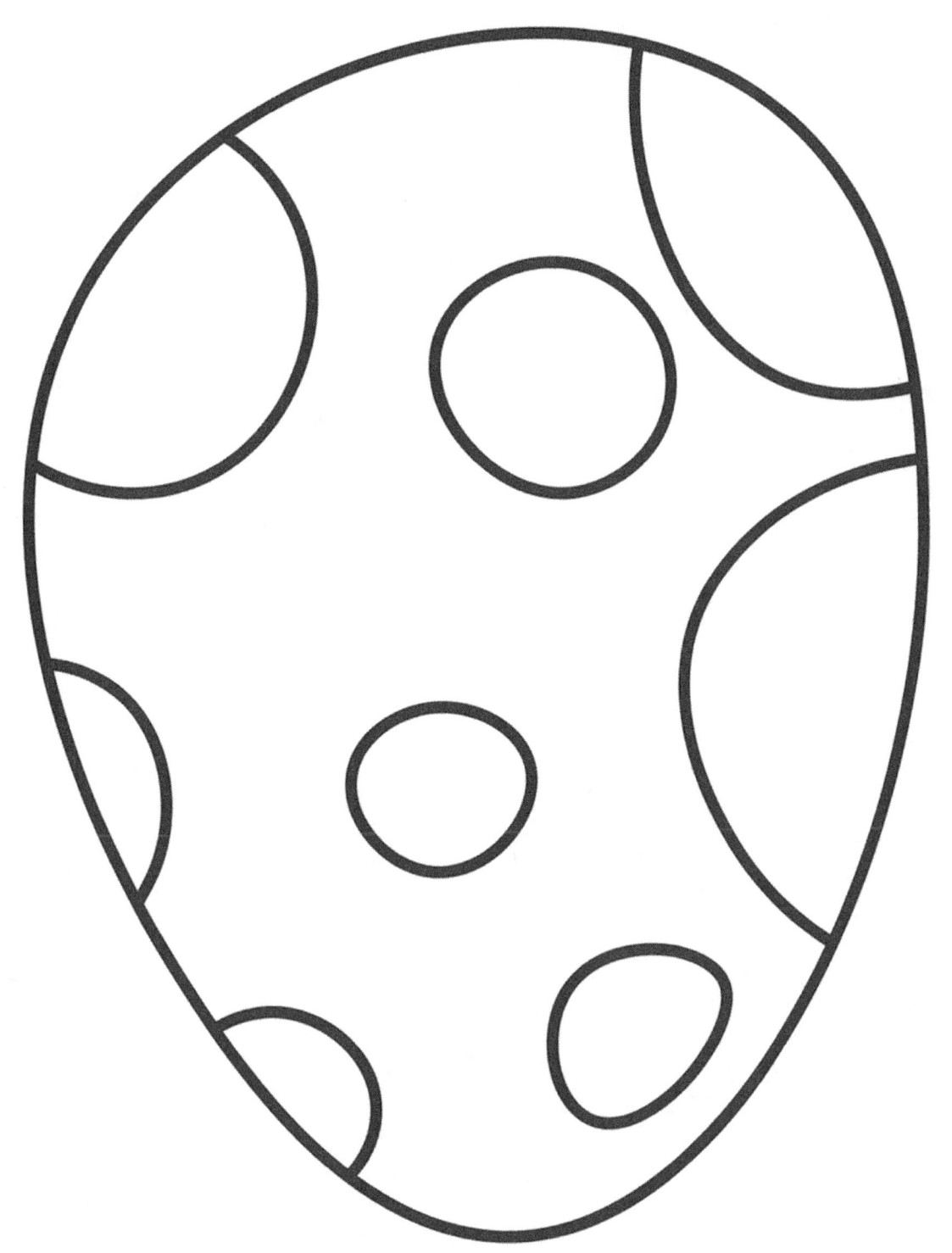

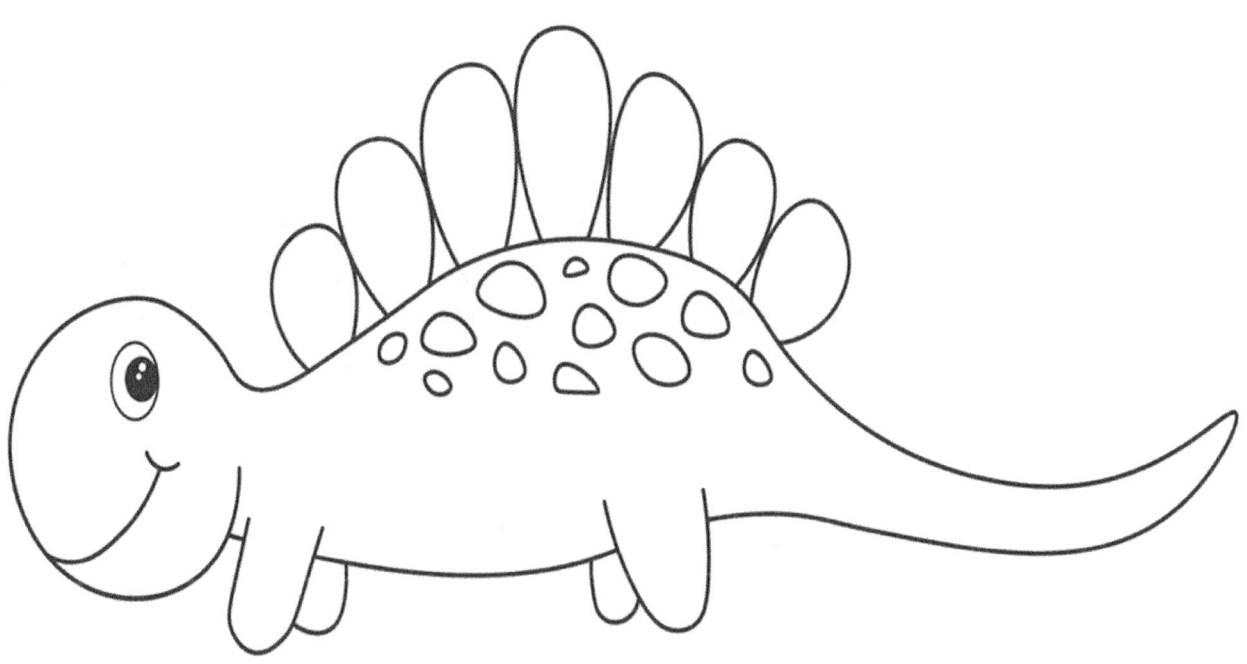

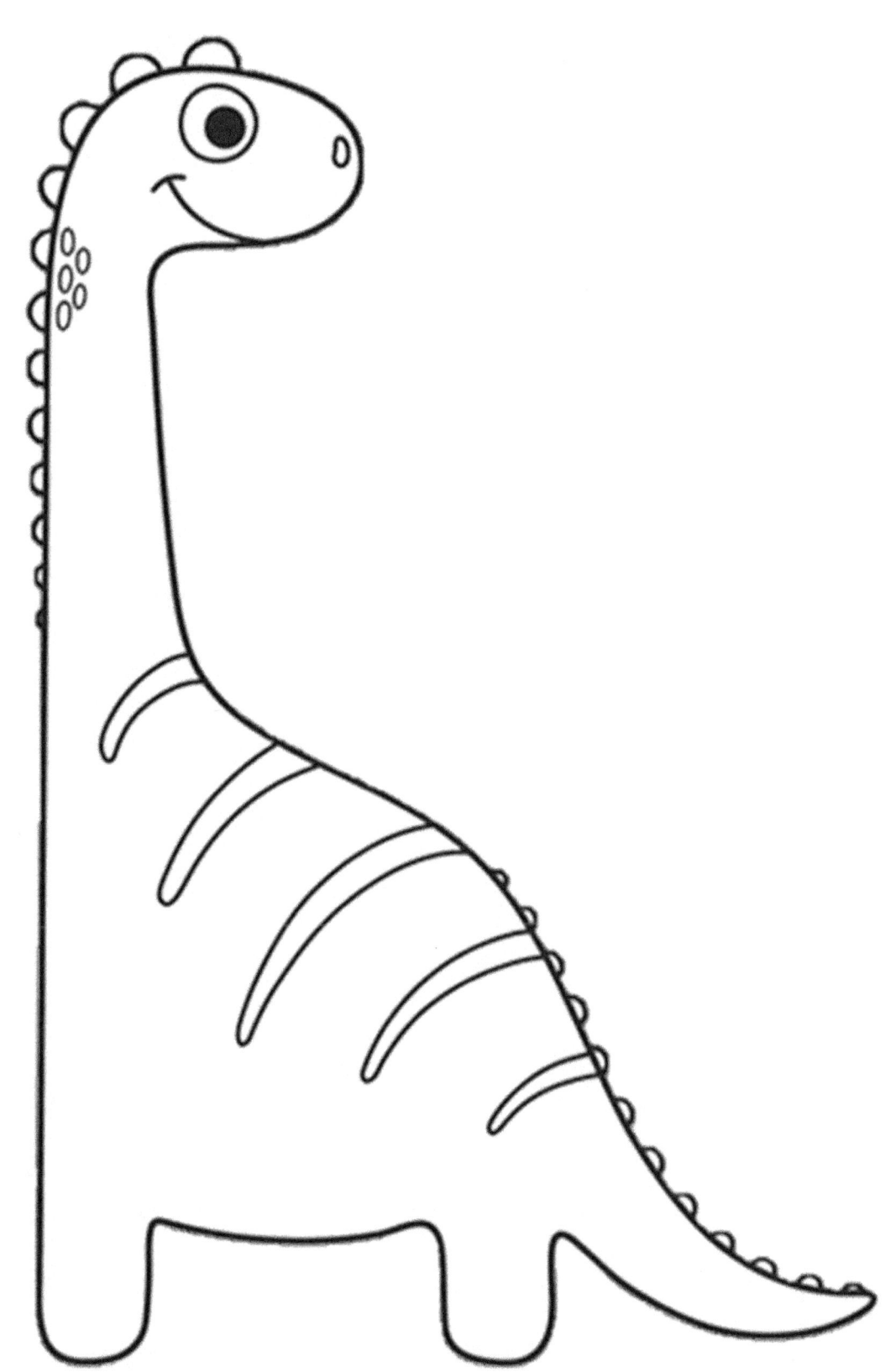

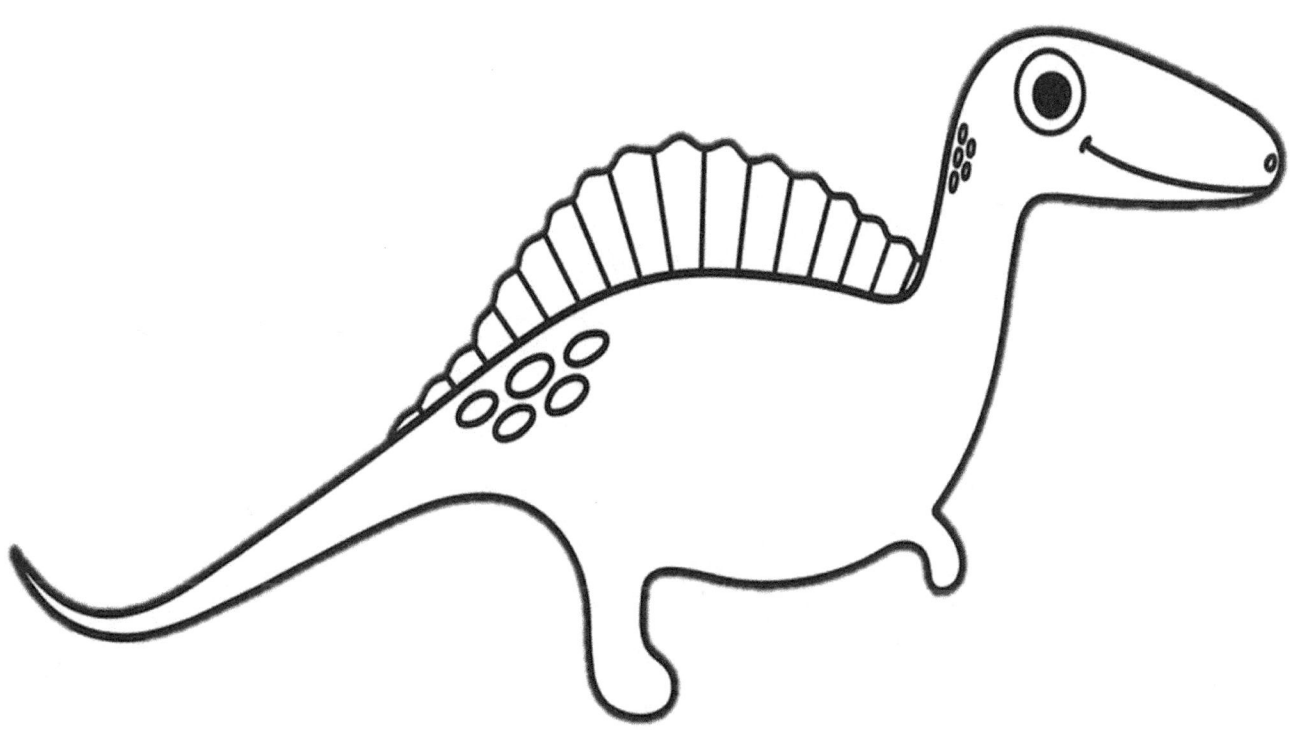

www.ingramcontent.com/pod-product-compliance
Lightning Source LLC
Chambersburg PA
CBHW052037280526
45791CB00010B/2993